WARTIME HARTLEPOO

by

Douglas R. P. Ferriday

Front cover: designed by Roy Hubbard

This book is dedicated to the people who lived through wartime Hartlepool and to those who lost their lives in times of conflict, in the hope that the future holds only peace and never again war.

First edition 1990
Published by Hendon Publishing Company Limited, Hendon Mill, Nelson, Lancashire, BB9 8AD

Printed by The Amadeus Press Ltd, Huddersfield, West Yorkshire, HD2 1YJ

The First World War

War has been a feature throughout Hartlepools' long history, firstly with the Scots, Danes and Normans and latterly the Germans. Hartlepool was to play prominent parts in two wars, particularly the Great War, 'War to end all wars', for on Wednesday, 16 December 1914, at seven minutes past eight in the morning the infamous bombardment took place. This was the first serious attack upon British soil and will be handed down in the annals of time as a callous and cowardly attack on civilians.

The bombardment lasted a full 35 minutes in which time 127 people were killed and over 400 seriously injured, many of them young children preparing for school.

The first soldier killed on British soil in the war met his fate during the bombardment, his name being Private Theo. Jones of the 18th Battalion D.L.I. and the first war distinction to be awarded on British soil went to Sgt. T. Douthwaite R.A. who received the Military Medal. All through the engagement the Heugh and Lighthouse Batteries under the command of Colonel L. Robson C.M.G., D.S.O., V.D., T.D., J.P., D.L. kept the enemy under constant fire, inflicting thirty casualties aboard the German armoured cruiser *Blucher*, later to be sunk in the North Sea by the British fleet, attempting another similar raid on 24 January 1915, the *Von der Tann* suffered severe damage and the *Seydlitz* was hit. Much damage was inflicted on the two towns including St Hildas Church, the Baptist Chapel, the Public Library, Prissick and Hart Road Schools, Richardson & Westgarths engineering works, the cement works, the tram depot, Irvines shipyard, ships in the docks and the gasworks, in addition to hundreds of houses throughout the Hartlepools.

Many tales are told of the bravery and experiences during the bombardment, one such memory of a child at the time relates, 'there was a loud knocking on the front door, and when my mother opened it, there was a woman covered in blood asking for help. At that moment across the fields I saw a great blaze, it appeared it was the gas works tanks next to the tram shed which were on fire. On coming downstairs I saw the glass had gone from the windows and the venetian blinds were blown to the ceiling, my mother brought the woman in and as there was no hot water did the best she could and finally wrapped the woman in a bed sheet and some towels, by then a man in uniform took her away.' For this action the Germans issued a special medal to those taking part. However the greater reward went to the people of Hartlepool and West Hartlepool who in spite of their severe battering were never defeated in either spirit or body, this action only reinforcing their determination and vigour.

Later in the war on Monday, 27 November 1916 at around a quarter to twelve in the morning a Zeppelin of the *Schutte Lang* type, 485 feet long, made an historic air raid on the Hartlepools. However the searchlights soon picked it out and 13 bombs were hastily released near Elwick village.

Flying at 10,000 feet the airship was attacked by anti-aircraft gun fire and aeroplanes. Four further bombs were dropped behind West Park and two in Ward Jackson Park damaging Tunstall Manor.

Fire broke out on the aircraft and bombs dropped haphazardly falling on Hartley Street, Lothian Road, Poplar Grove, Rugby Terrace and on allotments behind Victoria football field.

The Zeppelin now in flames headed out over St Hildas and fell into the sea a thousand yards from the shore, sinking in 40 fathoms. A total of 29 bombs were released and damage done to 554 houses and shops, although with no recorded casualties.

Credit for the destruction of the Zeppelin was given to Lieut. I. V. Pyott of the Royal Flying Corps. assisted by ground fire from the anti-aircraft guns. Further raids took place before the war was finally over, with more damage and casualties.

Zeppelin raids on the Hartlepools, Monday, 27 November 1916. Caught in the searchlights and in flames just before crashing into the sea off the Headland.

The third Zeppelin raid on 13 March 1918 causing much damage in Temperance Street, West Hartlepool, where four persons were killed.

Baptist Chapel Hartlepool. After the Bombardment on Wednesday, 16 December 1914.

Rear of the Baptist Chapel where the shell made its exit.

Bombardment 16 December 1914, Moor Terrace showing some of the severe damage to houses by shells from the German fleet.

German ships taking up position and retiring.

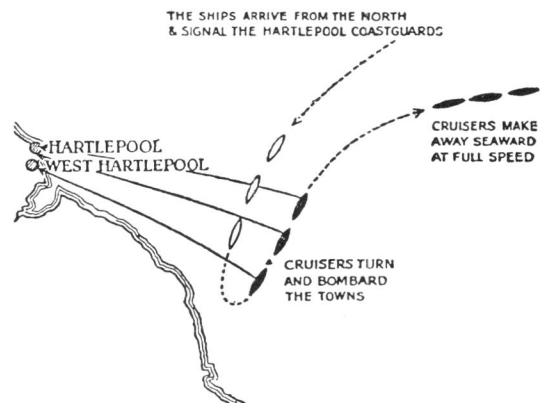

THE SHIPS ARRIVE FROM THE NORTH
& SIGNAL THE HARTLEPOOL COASTGUARDS

HARTLEPOOL
WEST HARTLEPOOL

CRUISERS MAKE
AWAY SEAWARD
AT FULL SPEED

CRUISERS TURN
AND BOMBARD
THE TOWNS

Damage to Irvine's shipyard, West Hartlepool.

PROCLAMATION.

The Inhabitants of West Hartlepool

Are requested to quietly pursue their usual work.

The message sent round this morning was due to a misunderstanding.

There is no cause for alarm.

J. R. FRYER, Mayor.

GOD SAVE THE KING!

PROCLAMATION.

NAVAL BOMBARDMENT.

The civil population are requested, as far as possible, to keep to their houses for the present. The situation is now secure. The Group Leaders of Each Ward will advise in case of further danger.

Any unexploded shell must not be touched, but information as to the position thereof given to the nearest Policeman or to the Police Station.

Dated, 16th December, 1914.

J. R. FRYER, Mayor.

GOD SAVE THE KING.

George Jopling, aged 77, 4, Dock Street, just after the Bombardment. His home was practically demolished yet he refused to leave his cosy kitchen fireside.

Shell damage to York Road and Poplar Grove, West Hartlepool.

Dene Street, West Hartlepool, on the day of the Bombardment. Ten people were killed here.

Two of the innocent victims of the Bombardment, Ralph Watts and Norman Edmundson, one losing a leg, the other an arm.

Unexploded shells with men of the Green Howards outside Staincliffe House, Seaton Carew.

Men of the R.G.A. and Durham R.G.A. (T) who manned the Hartlepool Gun Batteries on the 16 December 1914.

"A GLORIOUS VICTORY!"?

Translation:
Bombardment of Scarborough and Hartlepool by German Cruisers, 16th December, 1914.

Translation:
"GOD BLESS OUR UNITED ARMIES."

Silver Medal issued in Germany.

Silver medals issued by the Germans to commemorate 'A Glorious Victory'.

War Bond raising outside the Municipal Buildings, West Hartlepool. On the tank are the Mayor and Mayoress of West Hartlepool, the Mayor of Hartlepool together with Lady Londonderry and Mr Havelock Wilson. The sum raised in bonds for the Hartlepools was a magnificent £2,367,333. As a thank-you gesture, the tank 'Egbert' was presented to the town in 1919 and was displayed on Stranton Garth, Vicarage Gardens until taken for scrap during the Second World War.

Certificate awarded to Private Francis James Horsley for war service between 30 September 1916 and 28 October 1919 as a volunteer in the Durham Light Infantry.

Volunteer Force

To

N 334159 Pte Francis James Horsley.

I am commanded by The King to express to you His Majesty's thanks for the services which you have rendered to the Nation during the great War as an enrolled Volunteer in the

6th V. Bn The Durham Light Infantry

Winston S. Churchill

Secretary of State for War.

Certificate of Service

Enrolled 30 9 16   Discharged 28 10 1919

Entered into an Agreement under the Volunteer Act, 1916, on 20 3 17 to continue serving in the Force for the duration of the War, and to perform the prescribed programme of training.

Entered into an Agreement under the Volunteer Act, 1916, on _____ to perform temporary Service.

Served as a full-time soldier with a Volunteer Special Service Company from _____ 1918, to _____ 1918.

Thanks offering medal and flags to the Hartlepools' Hospitals in memory of the 16 December 1914. 'Ye did it to mine, Ye did it to me'

The Second World War

The Second World War in 1939, although less spectacular within the Hartlepools as the Great War, nevertheless left its mark on the town with suffering and damage to people and property.

During the air raids from the middle of 1940 up to early 1943 there were 43 sorties on the twin towns inflicting much material damage and a total of 70 fatalities (48 in West Hartlepool and 22 in Hartlepool).

There were 480 air raid warnings during the period. In West Hartlepool there were in addition 189 people injured and in Hartlepool 93.

Domestic and commercial areas were affected including Church Street: Edgar Phillips, The Yorkshire Bank and the Clarence Hotel, Musgrave Street: Central Hotel and St Joseph's School, Stockton Street: The Premier Hotel, The Greyhound Stadium and York Road.

One of the worst raids took place on the night of 19 August 1941 when a mine fell in Houghton Street and Elwick Road killing 38 people and injuring 70 others.

Nine lives were lost on 30 August 1940 during the early morning when bombs fell on Pilgrim Street and Hilda Street. Nineteen houses were destroyed and 120 damaged. The Headland also suffered severe loss of life on 12 May 1941. Perhaps it should be noted that in the 1914 bombardment, 127 lives were lost in just 50 minutes, whereas there were 43 raids over three years in the second war.

The nervous strain was enormous during such a long period, however the people of Hartlepool withstood the ordeal with the resolute will expected of them.

During 1939, the Emergency Committees were set up in anticipation of war being declared with 'trial' blackouts, the issue of gas masks and filling of sandbags to help protect buildings.

Children were evacuated to safer parts of the region, when war was declared in September 1939, the town, along with others throughout the country was reasonably prepared for the onslaught yet to come. In fact, 1,500 air raid wardens were trained and ready within months after the outbreak of war. Everyone, civilian and service alike waited for the expected invasion by sea and air, which never came yet remained in people's thoughts throughout the war. In 1940 the Battle of Britain was in full swing and West Hartlepool became one of the first industrial towns to receive German bombs on the evening of 19–20 June. Four falling in the Musgrave Street–Whitby Street area killing two, injuring 63 and causing great damage to this densely populated part of the town. In total 234 properties were either damaged or destroyed in this first raid. Four bombs fell on Gunners Vale Farm, Elwick, demolishing the farmhouse there.

In the Musgrave Street area 'people fumbled and stumbled about in the darkness, salvaging furniture, searching for relatives, or just giving a hand to anyone who needed it. There was no panic, no whining, and very few grumbles.' In the half-light of dawn someone spotted a half-naked woman seemingly beckoning for help from the shattered window of a shop. Help reached her in less than a single minute – but 'she' turned out to be a window model dummy, minus one arm and clothes.

It was business as usual next day wherever possible, for little inconveniences like air raids were not going to interfere with the normal working life of the people of Hartlepool if they could help it.

In the action the first British civil defence worker, Mr John Punton, aged 54, was killed.

During the summer of 1940 air raid alerts were sounded almost every day and night, sometimes lasting from dusk to dawn. In four months there were 147 alerts and on some days warnings numbered five or six, causing many people to sleep in the air raid shelters whether there was a raid on or not.

The first incendiary bombs, some 150, fell during July 1940, fortunately they were off target causing no damage or casualties. Most of the bombs in the very early days fell on grassland near to Graythorp, however the German High Command official communiqué stated 'Arms factories at Billingham and Newcastle were extensively damaged'.

By the end of July the raids became more accurate and aggressive inflicting severe damage and some casualties in the Throston Street–Stockton Street area. The Tin Box factory, Browns Sawmills, The Premier Hotel, C.M. Yuill-Villiers Street all received damage.

Rest Centres were established in the Presbyterian Church, Park Road and the Salvation Army Citadel, Stockton Street.

Many instances of courage, determination and wit are recorded and the people of Hartlepool generally went about their business as usual, ignoring as far as possible the real war about them.

On 26 August 1940 when Church Street was hit after near misses on the beach, Edgar Phillips advertised that 'business would be carried on as usual in John Street' and the Yorkshire Bank transferred to the Tower Street Baptist Church schoolrooms.

April 1941 saw the village of Graythorp extensively damaged, although there were few casualties, 74 houses were damaged as was the Co-op stores, the school and Mission Hall.

Due to an unexploded bomb, the whole village was evacuated and emergency billeting arrangements made at the Presbyterian Hall, Park Road. The villages around Hartlepool, particulary Elwick, were frequent targets for some strange reason. Whether they were thought to be munitions factories or simply 'missed' targets is not too clear.

During the raids the Police Force was constantly in attendance and it may be appropriate to mention P.C. Frederick White, a war reserve constable at the time, who earned an official commendation for brave conduct. The *London Gazette* stated, 'while these persons were being rescued, bombs were still falling in the vicinity, and the noise created by the guns and bombs added to the difficulty of the work. During the whole of the time enemy planes were overhead and high explosive and incendiary bombs were being dropped'. This was typical of the duties carried out by the force, for they were also rightly described as 'Jacks of All A.R.P. Trades' – that is warden, fireman, rescue, first–aid man and friends to anyone in distress.

The latest German High Command issue for 8 May 1941 states, 'Further effective air attacks were directed against Hartlepool, Middlesbrough, Bristol and Plymouth.' However that same night 23 enemy planes were shot down, making a total of 67 for the first seven nights of May.

In the early morning of 12 May 1941 a bomb fell on Lumley Square killing 12 people including all the members of one family, 25 people were also injured in the raid. An injured licensee returning to find his pub damaged promptly displayed a note to the effect, 'Still no cigarettes or spirits, but we are open as usual with beer at 11.30'.

The year 1941 was not a good one for the Hartlepools for on 19 August, the heaviest raid took place. In the Elwick Road area a mine exploded in back Houghton Street. Material damage was extensive including 91 houses and shops destroyed or damaged and 150 shop windows and another 200 houses slightly damaged.

Other areas which suffered in the same raid were Brenda Road, Haswell Avenue, Brierton, Owton Grange, and near to Greatham. Miss Lilly Dawson, a volunteer warden received injuries from which she died, being the second air raid warden to lose her life helping others. Mr Frank Littlefair, of Elwick Road, a special constable, also lost his life in this raid together with his wife and three children. Mr Russell Doxford lost his wife and three children also, in addition to his own sight.

1942 was a quieter year with twelve raids accounting for ten fatalities. In 1943 there were six more raids up to 22 March with no reported casualties and slight damage done to property.

The last recorded air raids on the Hartlepools was on 22 March 1943, mainly incendiaries falling harmlessly on Seaton Snooks.

In acknowledgement of the work done by the 'Civilian' force the Northern Regional Commissioner for Civil Defence, Sir Arthur Lambert, visited Hartlepool on 16 November 1944 to say 'a big thank you' for a job well done. He added, 'I think we can all agree, that Civil Defence found that its greatest asset was in the ordinary people of our towns, who were always tough and cheerful and faced up to adversity in the true British spirit.'

Hartlepool, like so many towns and cities gave its all to the war effort, including personal sacrifice of life and limb. It was a necessity brought about by circumstances beyond local control and the people reacted magnificently. Yet all the death and destruction points to the over-riding folly of war in its concept.

Since those eventful days the people of Hartlepool have generously utilised that same 'true spirit' for peaceful means, conquering differing adversities in the same way.

First aid and nursing staff of the Church Close First Aid Post, Hartlepool Headland May 1940.

Auxiliary Fire Service, a 'Binns' van is requisitioned as an emergency ambulance.

The Anderson steel shelter issued to every home with a garden. Many of these lasted well after the war ended and some are still in use as garden sheds, for they were well made of heavy gauge galvanised steel. Much of the production of these shelters was from local steelworks.

Men of the Auxiliary Fire Service with a mobile pump.

Many shops and St Josephs R.C. School shown on the left were severely damaged on the 19–20 June 1940.

Musgrave Street, West Hartlepool. The Central Hotel where one woman was killed on the night of the 19–20 June 1940.

General view of Musgrave Street following the first air raid on the Hartlepools, 19–20 June 1940.

This was an anxious time for mothers as the distribution of babies' gas masks was speeded up. The babies, as in the picture, wondered what all the fuss was about, but their mothers looked on intently as volunteer workers demonstrated the fitting of the respirators.

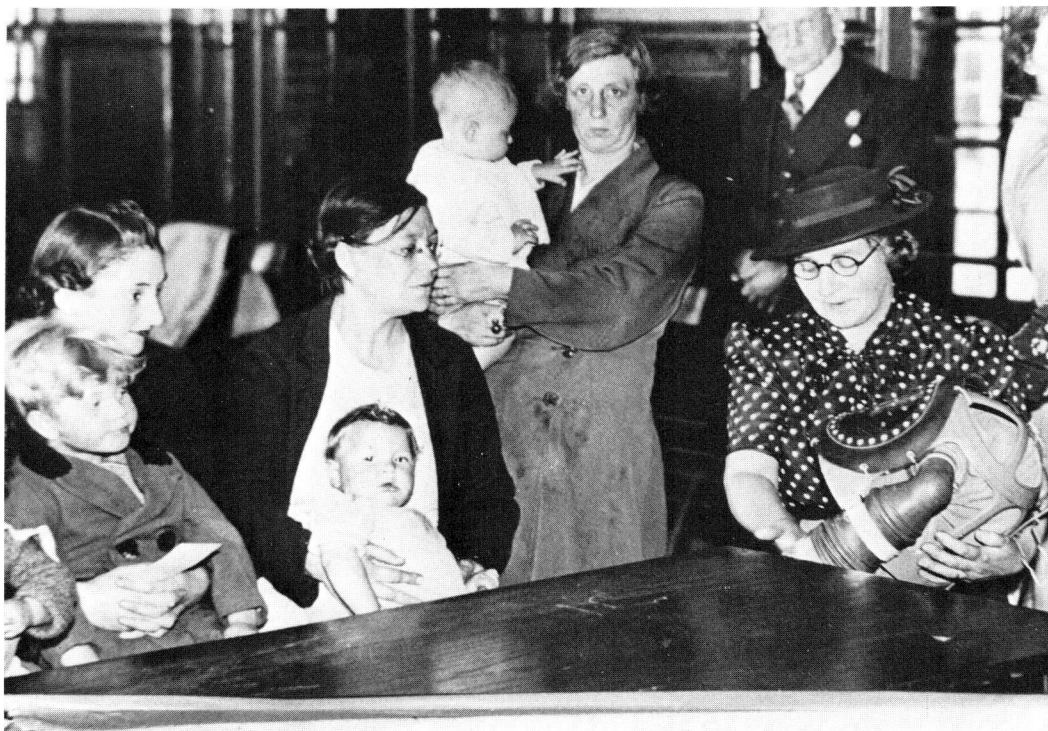

Hitler will send
no warning —
so always carry
your gas mask

ISSUED BY THE MINISTRY OF HOME SECURITY

View of Musgrave Street damage, 19–20 June 1940.

What was left of St Josephs School after the raid of 19–20 June 1940.

Soldier guarding the damaged and now empty houses in Musgrave Street area, June 1940.

Soldiers helping to clear away dangerous rubble after the June air raids.

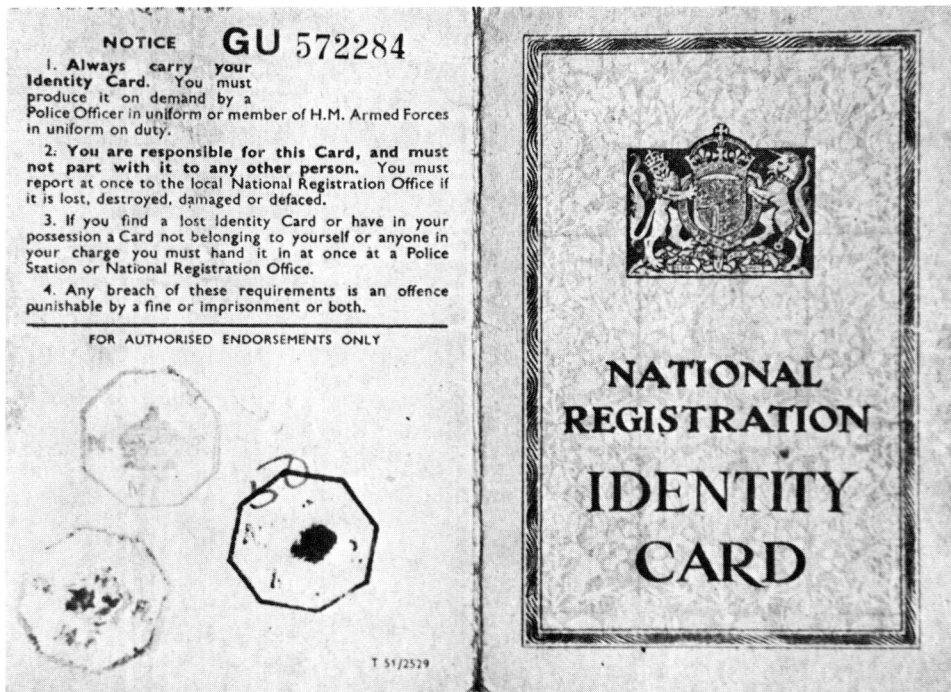

National Registration Identity Card. Issued during the war and had to be carried at all times, to be produced upon demand by police officers or H.M. Forces on duty.

Home Guard marching through the town.

Tin Boxes factory roof after the raid of 21 July, 1940.

Another view of the damage to the Tin Boxes factory after the raid on Thornton Street/ Villiers Street, 21 July 1940.

Damage to the rear of the Temperance Hotel, Stockton Street, 21 July 1940.

Buried beneath the wreckage of Edgar Phillips were two women and a man, near relatives, who lost their lives in the raid of 27 August 1940.

Church Street, two views of Edgar Phillips, the Yorkshire Penny Bank and the Clarence Hotel. Both the bank and the hotel were damaged and later demolished. Although the two photographs show the same scene in different moments the time remains the same, the clock stopped at ten minutes to one.

Brenda Road, West Hartlepool showing substantial damage following the raid of the 26 August 1940.

Faulder Road, West Hartlepool after the 26 August 1940 raid. The street is shown blocked with wreckage and furniture.

In the early days of the war, Air Raid Wardens made their posts at strategic points, including telephone kiosks, which may seem an odd arrangement, as this picture suggests to curious small boys.

Much war effort production took place at the steelworks. Armoured plate for ships and tanks was produced as well as many other steel products.

The Yorkshire Penny Bank, Church Street. Edgar Phillips next door received a direct hit at precisely 12.50 a.m. on the 27 August 1940.

A group of female workers at the South Durham Iron & Steel Co. Ltd., West Hartlepool 1940.

Pilgrim Street, West Hartlepool. Nine people lost their lives in a cellar on the 29 August 1940.

Damage to Hilda Street, West Hartlepool following the bombing of 30 August 1940.

Musgrave Street air raid damage, 30 August 1940.

The National Regional Chairman, Civil Defence Commissioner Sir Arthur Lambert (with bowler hat) at the scene of the Elwick Road/Houghton Street air raid of 19 August 1941. The Mayor Ald. O. Lupton is on Sir Arthur's right.

Two views of the bomb damaged West Hartlepool Greyhound Stadium following the raid on the 4 May 1941, when two fire watchers were trapped and killed.

Yorkshire Penny Bank and Edgar Phillips shop, Church Street, 27 August 1940.

Head Wardens and Fire Leaders, Hartlepool (Headland) Civil Defence Service.

HEAD WARDENS AND FIRE GUARD LEADERS - HARTLEPOOL CIVIL DEFENCE SERVICE
1939 - 1945

H. THOMAS	J. A. WATCHMAN	W. M. SCOTT	J. W. SWAN	W. H. SMITH	W. WILKINSON	J. WRIGHT	P. PEARSON
Asst. F.G.O.	District Head Warden	District Head Warden	District Head Warden	District Head Warden	S. Capt.	S. Capt.	S. Capt.
C. S. THEAKER	D. S. INNES	G. W. CHAINEY	W. C. POUNDER	G. E. CARTER	H. LISTER	T. E. WEATHERALL	W. DAVISON
District Head Warden	Head Warden	Head Warden	Head Warden	Head Warden	Head Warden	Head Warden	S. Capt.
C. CROFT	L. WILKINSON	MAJOR G. E. T. FULCHER	J. E. ROBINSON	W. J. COOK	P.C. P. WELLS	H. HUTCHINSON	
Area Capt.	Inspector of Police	A.R.P. Officer	(Chief Constable) Ch. Warden	Dep. Ch. Warden	Wardens' Staff Officer	Area Capt.	

With the Compliments of the Season

Our compliments and thanks to you all. For it is thanks very largely to you for so loyally and so helpfully working with us that at this, the fourth Christmas at war, the nation's health is on a sound footing. But though "good living" must now be taken in the sense of healthy living, instead of luxury living, and we all must go carefully with fuel, we can still make Christmas fare hearty, appetising and tempting to look at. Here, with our very best wishes, are some ideas which may help you:

❋ Christmas Day Pudding

Rub 3 oz. cooking fat into 3 tablespoonfuls self-raising flour until like fine crumbs. Mix in 1½ breakfastcupfuls stale breadcrumbs, ½ lb. prunes (soaked 24 hours, stoned, chopped) or any other dried fruit such as sultanas, 3 oz. sugar, 1 teaspoonful mixed spice, ½ teaspoonful grated nutmeg. Then chop 1 large apple finely, grate 1 large raw carrot and 1 large raw potato; add to dry ingredients. Stir in a tablespoonful lemon substitute. Mix 1 teaspoonful bicarbonate of soda in 3 tablespoonfuls warm milk and stir thoroughly into pudding mixture. Put into one large or two small well-greased basins, cover with margarine papers and steam for 2½ hours. This can be prepared overnight and cooked on Christmas Day.

❋ Emergency Cream

Bring ½ pint water to blood heat, melt 1 tablespoonful unsalted margarine in it. Sprinkle 3 heaped tablespoonfuls household milk powder into this, beat well, then whisk thoroughly. Add 1 teaspoonful sugar and ¼ teaspoonful vanilla. Leave to get very cold.

❋ Christmas Fruit Pies

This mixture is a good alternative to mincemeat.

Warm 1 tablespoonful marmalade (or jam, but this is not so spicy) in small saucepan over tiny heat. Add ¼ lb. prunes (soaked 24 hours, stoned, chopped) or other dried fruit, 1 tablespoonful sugar, 1 teacupful stale cake crumbs, or half cake, half breadcrumbs, ½ teaspoonful mixed spice. Stir together until crumbs are quite moist. Remove from heat, add 1 large chopped apple; also some chopped nuts if you have any. Make up into small pies, or large open flans. The mixture keeps several days in a cool place.

❋ Stuffed Mutton *With apple or bread sauce, this is as delicious as any turkey!*

1 leg of mutton, or loin of mutton (half a leg does, but is more difficult to stuff). Bone with a sharp carving knife and small kitchen knife, or get your butcher to do it. Spread the meat flat, stuff one end with your favourite savoury stuffing, one end with sausage meat, the two meeting in the centre. Fold meat over, re-forming into shape, sew with sacking-needle and stout thread, place sewn side down in baking dish, spread liberally with dripping. Put halved potatoes, peeled or in jackets, in the baking dish. Allow about 40-50 minutes before joint is done.

ISSUED BY THE MINISTRY OF FOOD (S50)

❋ Don't waste elsewhere the fuel you save at home.

No. 2 Area Training School, Auxiliary Fire Service, based at Wynyard Park, 7 June 1943.

Auxiliary Fire Service, Area Training School, Staff of No. 2 Fire Service at Scalby Manor, Scarborough, August 1944. Many of the officers were from the Hartlepools.

Barrage Balloons, operated by the R.A.F. were a familiar sight over Hartlepool and the Tees. Wire cables suspended below the balloons were intended to discourage low-flying aircraft.

SALUTE THE SOLDIER
SAVE MORE LEND MORE

Some of the evacuees from wartime Hartlepool on a day out from Scarborough where they were billeted.

Auxiliary Fire Service drill practice on the sandbags.

Auxiliary Fire Service during fire drill practice. The men are wearing respirators at the ready.

Auxiliary Fire Service, Section 'D' at St Aidans School, West Hartlepool.

Barnard Street Fire Station as it was in wartime. Specially adapted vehicles were assembled to cope with the demands of war. This picture is towards the end of the war in early 1945.

West Hartlepool Ambulance Service around 1945. Splendid work was carried out throughout the war by this much appreciated band of workers

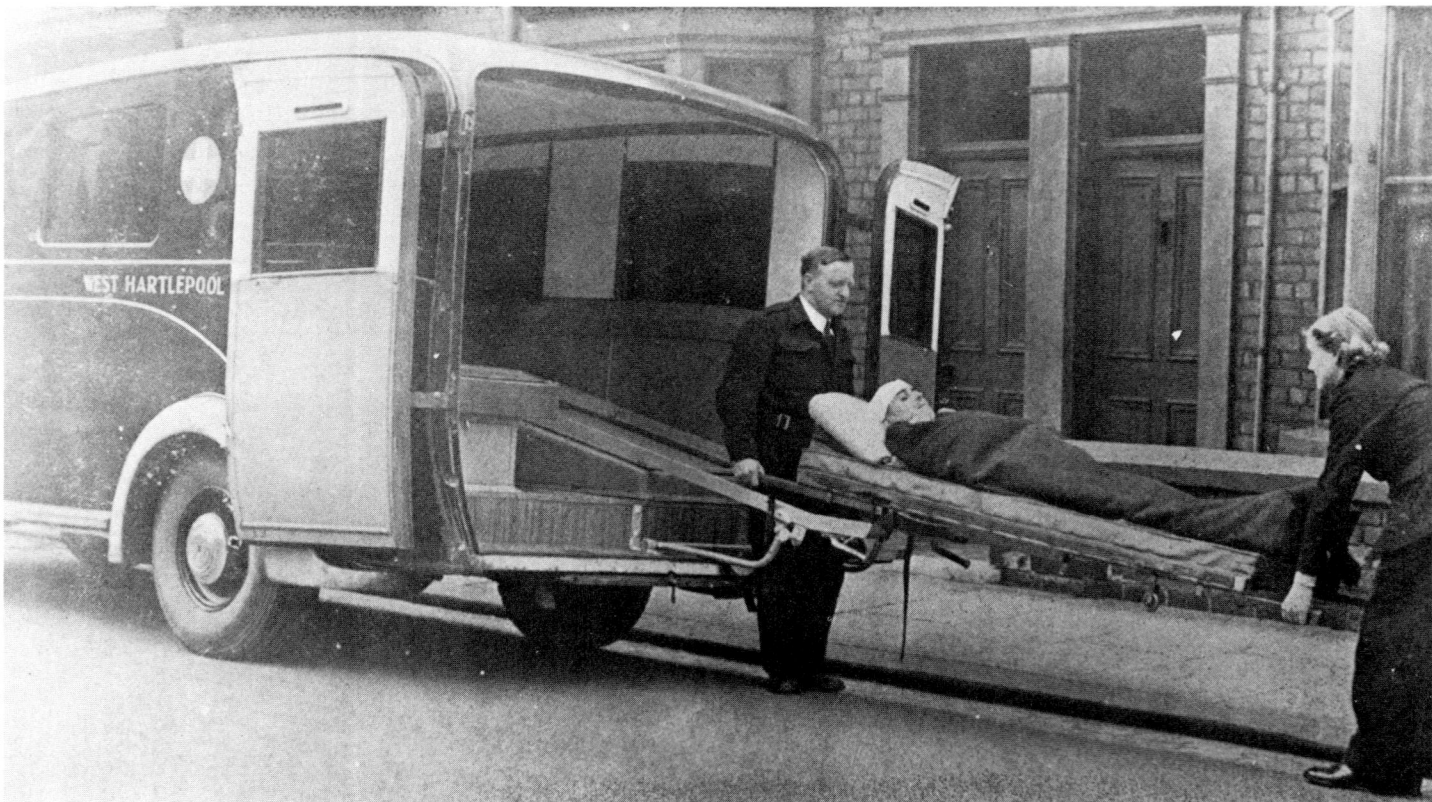

Members of the town Home Guard on Victory Square, West Hartlepool, with the Cenotaph in the background. Houses in South Road can be seen on the left. The large white houses are now occupied by Perry's, Victoria Road.

The Home Guard Band consisting of the peacetime West Hartlepool Old Operatic Band, who all volunteered to serve, thus providing a ready-made band. Seated third from the left is Sgt. Major William H. Saunders the conductor.

GB 4512 bc mit 4513 bc (2. Ang.)

Nur für den Dienstgebrauch! FOR THE USE OF SERVICES PERSONNEL ONLY
Bild Nr. 2949 Z 45 V.

Aufnahme vom 9. 3. 43

West Hartlepool
Hafenanlagen

Länge (westl. Greenw.): 1° 12′   Nördl. Breite: 54° 41′ 45″
Zielhöhe über NN: —

Lfl. Kdo. 3   August 1943

Karte 1:100000
GB/E 3

500   0   500   1000 m
Maßstab 1:14 000

A

N

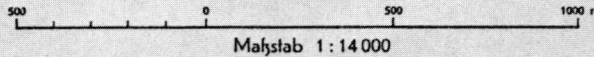

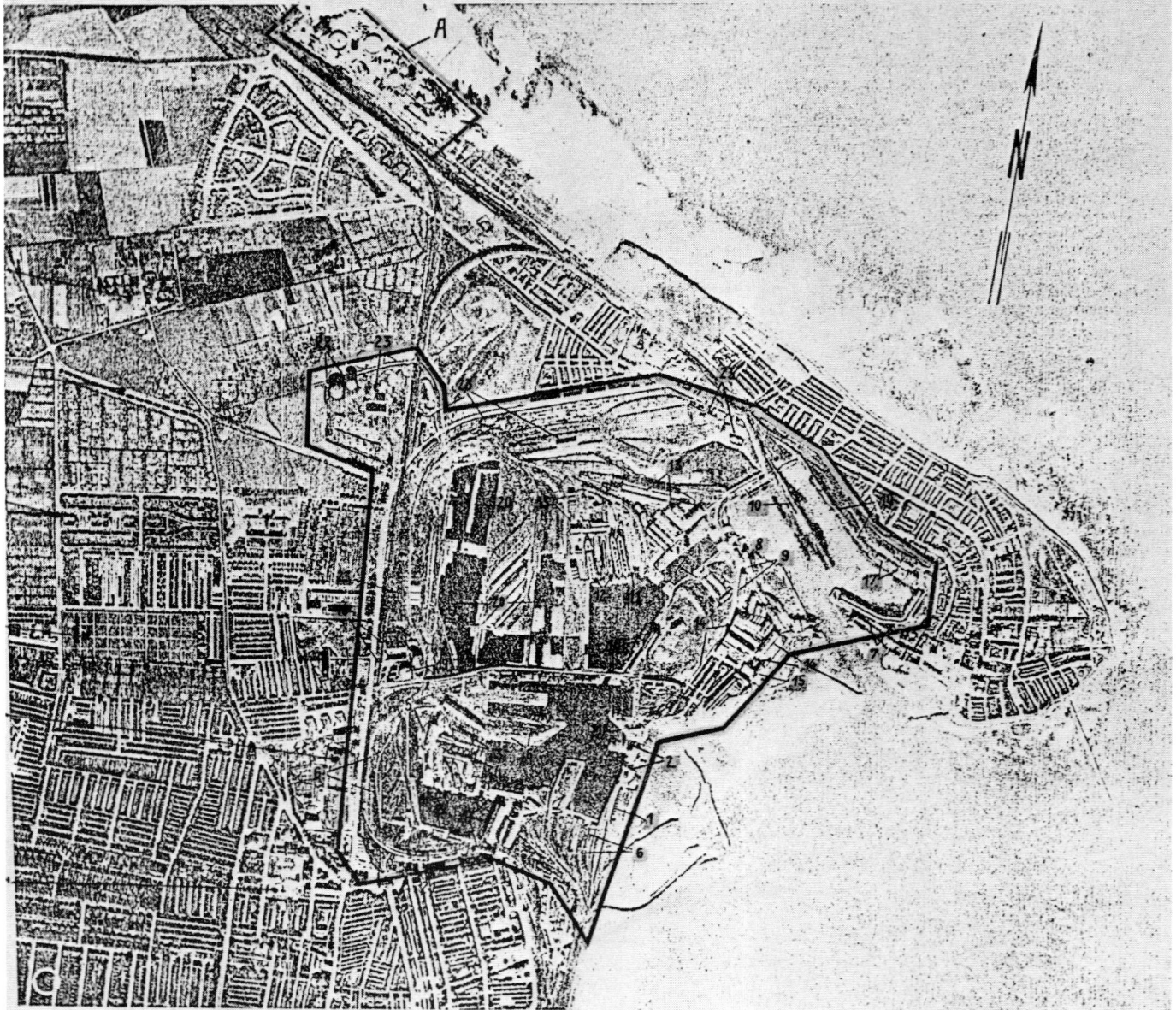

45 12 Südhafen
1. Lager-, Verwaltungs- u. Nebengebäude   etwa   11 600 qm
2. 2 Flutschleusen mit Betriebshaus   etwa   250 qm
3. 4 Hellinge
4. 2 Trockendocks, etwa 100 u. 115 m lang
5. Schiffsbauhallen u. Werkstätten   etwa   9 000 qm
6. Umschlagplätze u. Verladeanlagen

45 13 Nordhafen
7. Lagergebäude   etwa   14 000 qm
8. Trockendock, etwa 115 m lang
9. Werkstatthallen   etwa   2 600 qm
10. Umschlagplätze u. Verladeanlagen

83 11 Schiffswerften am Südhafen
11. Trockendock, etwa 165 m lang
12. 5 Hellinge
13. Schiffsbauhallen u. Werkstätten   etwa   41 000 qm
82 11 Maschinenfabriken Hartlepool-Middleton
14. Fabrikhallen, Verwaltungs- u. Nebengebäude   etwa   42 500 qm
15. Kraftstation   etwa   1 500 qm
56 20 Kühlhaus am Südhafen
16. Kühlhäuser u. Lagergebäude   etwa   3 600 qm
56 19 Kühlhäuser am Fischereihafen
17. 10 Lagerschuppen, Kühlhäuser u. Nebengebäude etwa   4 400 qm

52 58 Gaswerk
18. Kokerei u. Nebengebäude   etwa   4 300
19. Gasbehälter, etwa 39 m ∅
20. Docks zur Holzlagerung
21. Bahnhof
22. 2 Gasbehälter, etwa 31 m ∅ u. 42 m ∅
23. Sonstige Lager- u. Hafengebäude   etwa   12 000
Bebaute Fläche   etwa   146 750
Gesamtfläche   etwa 2 240 000
A Fabrikanlage zur Verarbeitung tierischer Fette
Gleisanschlüsse zu allen Anlagen vorhanden

A map of West Hartlepool (including Hartlepool) produced by German Intelligence in August 1943. Maps like this were produced of all major potential targets throughout the U.K. and would have been used to plot bombing raids as in this instance the docks, shipyards and railways.

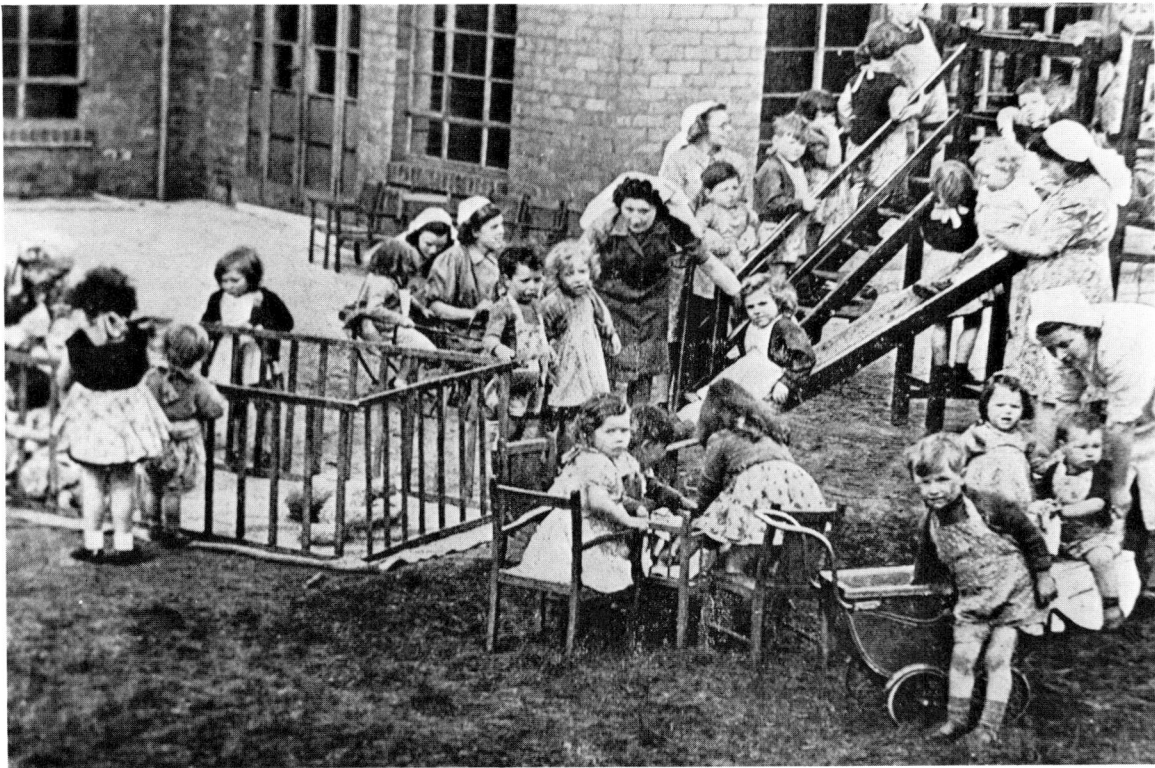

By the end of the war day nursery facilities were well established. This is the Grantully Day Nursery in 1945 – not too many smiling faces!

No. 104 Heavy Anti-Aircraft Battery (Ack–Ack) of the Home Guard who manned the Rocket Battery on the Headland Town Moor in 1944. The picture shows the officers and N.C.Os of just one of the platoons involved in manning the Battery. Some of the members of this formal group are Capt. Rammage; Sgt. Major Alderson; Sgt. Taylor; Sgt. Benvin; Sgt. Hale; Sgt. Blackett; Sgt. Baister; Bombardier Goodchild; and Bombardier (Cpl) Leo Gillen at the extreme right front row.

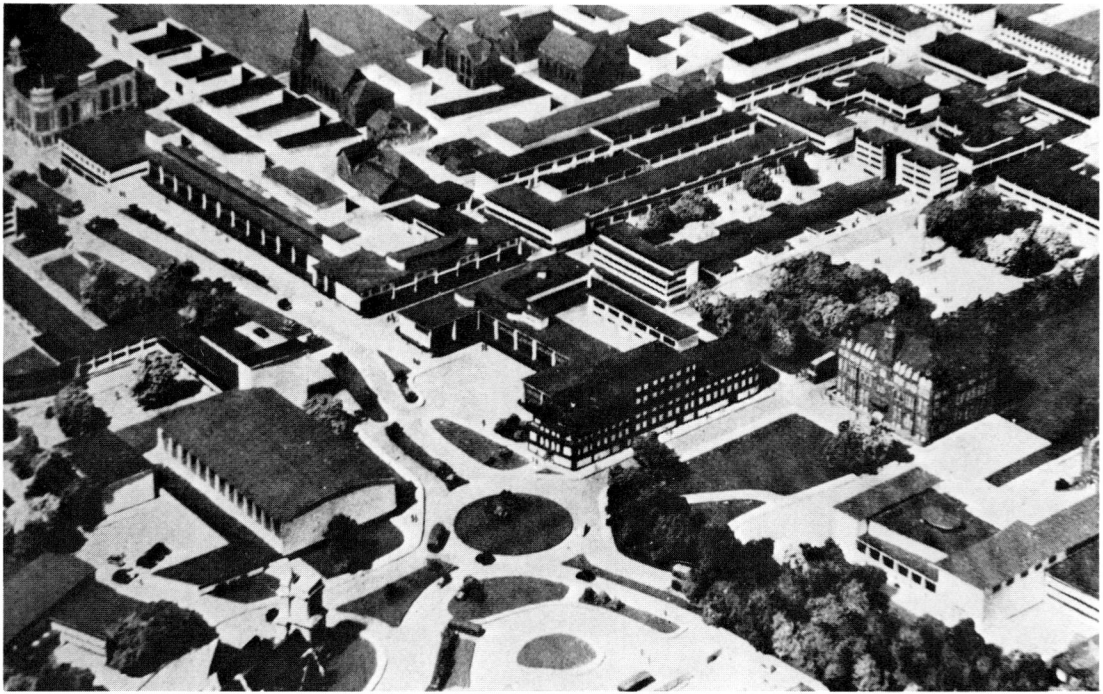

This aerial photograph of 1946 shows the area almost as it had been pre-war. After the war was finally over, great plans were made to rebuild the twin towns 'fit for heroes to live in' and Max Lock was commissioned to design the Hartlepools of the future.

Models were made depicting the radical changes to be made, and as the two photographs show, both West Hartlepool town centre (Max Lock) and Hartlepool Headland were to undergo major changes. Some of the ideas were implemented in the 1960s and the amalgamated town of Hartlepool continues to change today, sometimes for the better, but unfortunately not always so.

HEADLINE FASHIONS OF 1945.

The Docks and Harbour system survived the war. What little damage inflicted was repaired quickly.

NYLONS

EARL.

"THEY'VE CHANGED THEIR TUNE NOW THE WAR IS OVER, HAVEN'T THEY ETHEL"

The West Hartlepool Spitfire

During the dark days following the fall of France every citizen of the British Isles wished to play their part in the war effort. One of the simplest and most effective ways was to contribute to a National Fund. However, people wanted to identify with their donations and with the Battle of Britain about to commence in 1940 it was considered suitable to contribute towards the purchase of a fighter aircraft, preferably a Spitfire, which had captured the public imagination. A nominal figure of £5,000 was suggested to buy a Spitfire and so the Fund started throughout the land.

West Hartlepool's Spitfire Fund soon reached the required figure. On the 9 August 1940 a batch of 450 Spitfire Mk 1s were ordered and in February 1941 one of these, No.R7132 was decorated with the town crest and given the name *Industria*.

Although not in the actual Battle of Britain this aircraft saw active service with No.124 Squadron R.A.F. from Castletown, Caithness, protecting North Atlantic convoys and dealing with German aircraft operating from occupied Norway. When the Squadron moved to Biggin Hill later in 1941 *Industria* was left behind and used for training purposes.

After much use and repair the aircraft was sent to the Mediterranean theatre of war where she served until March 1944, then discarded and written off after surviving much longer than most of the Mk 1s. In fact, four years service rather than the usual life span of less than three months.

West Hartlepool's *Industria* certainly gave value for money and the people who donated to its cost were justly proud of this record.

As the first pilot of the aircraft, Derek S. Yapp, recorded in his log, 'I see from my log book that I made 100 flights in R7132, all without mishap or so much as a cough from the engine'.

DIG FOR VICTORY

Some wartime dates of interest.

1939

Hart Road Methodist Church built, and the Brus Arms opened.

23 August: trial blackout introduced.

1940

15 August: a Hurricane Fighter aircraft, No. P2717, belonging to 605 Squadron force lands at Hart Station.

12/13 September: bombs fell on the West View area killing one man and injuring two children.

1941

16 March: two high–explosive mines drop in the sea just off Marine Drive. 500 houses damaged and nine people received slight injuries.

6/7 May: two mines fall on the Palliser Works which at that time also came under Government ownership.

Concrete observation tower built in the lighthouse enclosure.

12 May: bombs fall on the Headland, killing twelve people injuring twenty-nine in Lumley Square.

21 July: H.R.H. The Princess Royal christened the new lifeboat in her name.

1942

January: visit by H.R.H. The Duke of Kent.

R.N.L.I. crew receive medals for service at the wreck of the *Hawkwood*.

September: Hartlepools Hospital extension opened.

12 December: bombs fall on Central Estate, one hitting the Central United Club. Nine people were killed in Union Road.

14 December: bombs dropped on Hart Station, the Golf Links and Middleton Foreshore.

Temporary school opened at West View.

1943

Col. T.G. Greenwood elected Member of Parliament for the Hartlepools.

Hartlepool Athletic Rugby Football Club is formed.

1944

8 May: Tipperary club and St Johns Church, Brougham Street burnt down.

11 July: the local and well–known singer Chick Henderson reported killed during an air raid on Portsmouth.

1945

8 May: V.E. (Victory in Europe) Day.

Durham County Education Authority take over Hartlepool schools.

David T. Jones elected M.P. for the Hartlepools.

Instructions on how to use this Book

1. The holder's name, full postal address and National Registration Number must be written in the spaces provided on page 1, in INK, before this book can be used.

2. When shopping, you must not cut out the coupons yourself, but must hand this book to the shopkeeper and let him cut them out. IT IS ILLEGAL FOR THE SHOPKEEPER TO ACCEPT LOOSE COUPONS.

3. When ordering goods by post, do not send this book—cut the coupons out, and send them with your order by registered post.

4. All clothing books of deceased persons must be handed to the Registrar of Births and Deaths when the death is notified.

5. If you are recalled to Service and have not obtained extra coupons against the application form on page 8, see that it is kept safely until your return to civilian life.

6. This book is the property of H.M. Government, and may only be used by or on behalf of the person for whom it is issued. TAKE GREAT CARE NOT TO LOSE IT.

Page 2

CLOTHING COUPON

CLOTHING COUPON

CLOTHING COUPON

CLOTHING COUPON

onal Registration No.

FOR OFFICIAL USE

Page 8